THE LOVE OF
LIBERTY
MET US HERE

THE P.R.C. STORY

ALEX DOUGBOWEA TARLUE

Copyright © 2023 Alex Dougbowea Tarlue.

All rights reserved. No part of this book may be reproduced, stored, or transmitted by any means—whether auditory, graphic, mechanical, or electronic—without written permission of both publisher and author, except in the case of brief excerpts used in critical articles and reviews. Unauthorized reproduction of any part of this work is illegal and is punishable by law.

ISBN: 979-8-88640-643-6 (sc)
ISBN: 979-8-88640-644-3 (hc)
ISBN: 979-8-88640-645-0 (e)

Because of the dynamic nature of the Internet, any web addresses or links contained in this book may have changed since publication and may no longer be valid. The views expressed in this work are solely those of the author and do not necessarily reflect the views of the publisher, and the publisher hereby disclaims any responsibility for them.

Theme: Peace, tranquility and the "pursuit of happiness" can not be achieve without understanding the ROOT of the problem.

One Galleria Blvd., Suite 1900, Metairie, LA 70001
1-888-421-2397

CONTENTS

Acknowledgements v

Chapter 1   Emergent, (Africa's Oldest Republic) 1

Chapter 2   From Colony to Republic. - (1820-1847) 7

Chapter 3   The Formation of the Defense Force 15

Chapter 4   Dynasty, Days of the Elites 21

Chapter 5   Birth of a New Era, P.R.C. 27

Chapter 6   People's Redemption Council Downfall 33

Chapter 7   New Beginning/ Old Wine in a New Bottle 39

Chapter 8   Destiny Unknown/ Are We There Yet 45

Chapter 9   Resolutions/ Recommandations 51

Author's Bio 55

ACKNOWLEDGEMENTS

1. David Komoh Tarlue
2. Ziah Nyanue
3. Kpadehee Tarlue
4. Joseph Sackor
5. Helena Powah
6. Edwina Mammie Kar
7. Eddi Robert Gaye, Jr.
8. Mary G. Saydee

Providence Island

CHAPTER ONE

EMERGENT, (AFRICA'S OLDEST REPUBLIC)

In the beginning before the land called Liberia was known to the Portugueses explorers who landed on the African Continent in 1462 - and name the piece of land now called (Liberia), Costa da Pimento meaning (Pepper Coast) or Grain Coast because of the abundance of melegueta pepper which became desired in European cooking. Few centuries later, after the Portugueses exploded Africa, slavery began. The first Africans to reach the colonies shores that England was struggling to establish were group of some 20 enslaved people who arrived at Point Comfort, Virginia, near Jamestown, in August 1619 brought by British privateers who had seized them from a captured Portuguese slave ship. The first Africans landed in Virginia British Colony in 1619. It was a turning point for slavery in the American History, but it was not the beginning. At the very least, 1619 represented a landmark in the long history of slavery in European colonies. America join in later after it's independent from Great Britain, (1776).

Throughout the 17th and 18th centuries people were kidnapped from the continent of Africa, forced into slavery in the American colonies and exploited to work as indentured servants and labor in the production of crops such as tobacco and cotton. In 1816 the American Colonization Society (ACS) was formed to send free African-Americans back to Africa as an alternative to emancipation in the United State. In 1822, the society established the West Coast of Africa a Colony that in 1847 became the independent nation called Liberia. The Republic of Liberia, formerly was a colony of the American Colonization Society, declares its independence later under pressure from Great Britain to set this negro republic free. United States hesitantly accepted the Liberian sovereignty, making the West African nation the first Democratic Republic in African history. A constitution modeled after the U.S. Constitution was approved, and in 1848 Joseph Jenkins Roberts was elected Liberia's first president.

The country was name Liberia meaning free from a latin word "Liberty" and city Monrovia was also name after American's President James Monroe, born (1758 - 1831), who was also the fifth U.S. President, who oversaw major westward expansion of U.S. and strengthened American foreign policy later on in 1923 with the Monroe = Doctrine, which also serve as a warning to European countries against further colonization and intervention in the Western Hemisphere. During his tender, he also supported the work of the American Colonization Society to create a home for freed African Slaves in Liberia. Before the settlers came to Liberia, the first inhabitants were ancestors of the Gola, and Kissi peoples from North-Central Africa who arrived as early as the 12th Century. They were joined by the Kruan people -(Kru, Kuwaa, Bassa, Krahn, and Dei Ethnic Groups) moving in from the north and east. When the first Colonies landed on the West Coast of Africa by (ACS), they could not find a place to unload except a small piece of Island on the Mesurado River that was later name Providence Island by the settlers. This Island play an important roll in the history of the United States and its relationship to Africa and people of African decent.

In 1822 the small Island at the mouth of the Mesurado River became one of the first places freed slaves from America landed and formed the nation of Liberia. This Island was originally called Dozoa, meaning "Land in the center of water" in the language of the the Gola ethnic groups.

Joseph Jenkins Robert, the first president of Liberia was born in Norfolk Virginia (USA) on (March 15, 1809- and died February 24,1876) emigrated to Liberia in 1829, where he became a noted politician. He first served as the governor to the settlers from (1841 to 1848) and then became elected as President from (1848 to1856) again he served (1872 to 1876). His contributions to Liberia was very valuable to this country. He also help shape the political land-scape of Liberia, and was very influential in the Foundation of Liberia. Liberians are indebted to this man for his enormous contribution to his people.

However, before the people of Liberia became one people, there were lot of things that took place between the settlers and the natives of Liberia. When the settlers first arrived on Providence Island, they had no clue of what to expect or what was ahead of them. The natives of the land were Bassa and Gola people apart from the other tribes people that were occupying the land, mostly in the remote part of the country. There are 16 ethnic groups that make up the Liberia's indigenous population besides the settlers. The indigenous African tribes that are 95% of the population are, (Kpelle, Bassa, Gio Kru, Grebo, Mandingo, Mano, Krahn, Gola, Gbandi, Loma, Kissi, Vai, and Bella) Americo -Liberians were 2.5%. (descendants of immigrants from the U.S.). Everything was separated at the time, the Settlers were on the Island and the natives were on the main land. Things were calm as long as they were separated, but yet both sides did not want things to remain like that. Because, before the arrival of the first batch of freed slaves from America, Providence Island was a major trade post for both Portuguese and ethnic groups of the land. When the settlers started occupying the Island, this became an issue for the natives. But after some amicable agreements, the natives decided to welcome the settlers because the natives felt these were bothers and sisters that were taken away and were brought back to their mother's land.

Things seem to be normal at the time, but conflict was brewing up between the two groups (settlers and natives). However, they went along with business as usual. The issues were acceptable between the two groups for some time (Natives and settlers). One of the issues was fear. Fear of domination and control of either one of the groups. Simultaneously, they both got along and co-existed for some times for few years. Yet and still the fear was always there between the two. The natives fear was, (who are these people and why the white men brought them here), even though they were their brothers and sisters that were taken away, but they are different now, with different ideology. So how will we fit into their company, into their minds, and their circle of friends and families. Those were the burning issues the natives were face with concerning the settlers. And on other hand, the settlers concerned was that, (the natives are bunch of "scavengers that are not civilized uneducated and has nothing to offer"). So, the line was drawn between the two groups separately, but co-existed in their own areas. Land ownership was unheard-of to the natives. They believed that where-ever you build your hut was your spot for you and your family. (buying land was strange to the Natives). Whatever the settlers brought with them to this African nation was so foreign to their way of life. The fear factors to the Natives was proven by the strange behavior of these settlers. Who are these people, they wonder.

Americo-Liberians / Settlers

Seal of Liberia

CHAPTER TWO

FROM COLONY TO REPUBLIC. - (1820-1847)

In 1820 the American Colonization Society sent its first group of immigrants to Sherbro Island in Sierra Leone. The Island swampy, unhealthy conditions resulted in a high death rate among the settlers as well as the society representatives. So the British governor allowed the immigrants to relocate to a safer area temporarily while ACS worked to save its colonization project from complete disaster. 1821 ACS dispatched a representative Dr. Eli Ayres to purchase land Father north up the cost from Sierra Leone. With the aid of U.S. Naval Officer, Lt. Robert F. Stockton, Ayres cruised the coastal waters west of Grand Bassa seeking out appropriate lands for the colony. At first the Dey and Bassa Chiefs were reluctant to surrender their peoples' land to the strangers, but were forcefully persuaded - some accounts were at gun-point to part with "36 mile long and and 3 mile wide" strip of coastal landforms trade goods, supplies, weapons and sum worth approximately $300.00. 2 years Later, April 25, 1822 the survivors of Sherbro Island arrived at Cape Mesurado and began to build their settlement. Through the years, ACS governed the colony through its representative. In time, however, some colonists objected strenuously to the authoritarian policies instituted by Jehudi Ashmum, (Methodist Missionary).

A methodist missionary who replaced Ayres as the ACS governing representative. Such disagreements created tensions within the struggling settlement. Believing that the colonial agent had allocated town (lots) and rationed provisions unfairly, a few of the settlers armed themselves and forced the society's representative to flee the colony. However, the disagreements were resolve after ACS representatives investigated the issues and persuaded Ashmun to return.

Slavery and participation in the slave trade were forbidden, also the settlement that used to be called Christopolis was rename Monrovia after American President, James Monroe, and the colony as a whole was called Liberia (the free land of liberty).

The colonies established by the Virginia Colonization Society, the Quaker Young Men's Colonization Society of Pennsylvania, and the American Colonization Society merged as the Commonwealth of Liberia and claimed control over all settlements between Cestos River and Cape Mount. The Commonwealth also adopted a new constitution and a newly-appointed governor in 1841. In 1842 The Mississippi Settlement at the mouth of the Sinoe River joined the Commonwealth that year. During that period up to 1846, the Commonwealth received most of is revenue from custom duties which angered the indigenous traders and British merchants on whom they were levied. The British government advised Liberian authorities that it did not recognize the right of the American Colonization Society, a private organization, levy these taxes. Britains refusal to recognize Liberian sovereignty convinced many colonists that independence with full taxing authority was necessary for the survival of the colony and its immigrant population. In October that year (1846) Americo-Liberian colonists voted in favor of independence. On July 26, 1847 the Liberian Declaration of Independence was adopted and signed. Under the leadership of governor (Joseph Jenkins Roberts), they called upon the International community to recognize the independence and sovereignty of Liberia. Britain was one of the first nations to recognize Liberia until the American civil War. 1847 - 1848. The Liberian Constitution was ratified and the first elections were held in the new republic, and Joseph Jenkins Roberts was elected first president of Liberia, (A Virginia born American). Subsequently after the election in the new republic, the nation needed to expand its territory, so land ownership was the next thing on the minds of the settlers. On the contrary, the natives did not know what is meant to own a land, all they knew was the land belongs to anyone and everyone who lives in that spot or that area. They had no clue of purchasing a land or land ownership. These things were very strange to the Chiefs and elders at the time. However, the settlers when ahead to request the Natives to give them some space or piece of land to build their homes. Because the settlers were anticipating more people to join them, more (settlers) to come and settle in Liberia, who the settlers referred to as brothers and sisters, including cousins, uncles and aunties that were to follow later over the years. "Go ahead pick a spot where ever you want,", responded by the Natives Chiefs. "You people are our brothers and sisters that taken away by the White people" The natives continue. "This is your land, you welcome to have as much as you want, in-fact, throw a rock wherever it lands is your spot". The Natives conceited. With the intention to show kindness and solidarity to the brothers and sisters that were once taken away by the white man as slaves.

Not knowing what may transpire in the near future, the settlers accepted the offers from the natives with excitements and appreciations. In so doing, the settlers made a counter offers to show their appreciation by supplying the Chiefs and Elders with Salts and Smoke Fish, as a token of gratitude for the kind gesture by the natives. Everybody was happy and things when normal for some time. But as the years when by, things started to changed, the settlers spaces were growing and growing, not only that, they were fencing their properties. They don't want their kids and natives kids to play together, because natives kids were not civilized "country" as they were referred to. Gradually, problems started to emerge, the natives got concerned and wanted to know what was going on. (unknown to the natives, the settlers were moving the rocks farther and farther away from the original spots). Causing chaos and confusion to the natives. "What is going on" they wonder. Again the settlers pretended as if nothing was happening, they proceeded to business as usual. "Nothing is going on" the settlers responded. (complete disregards to the natives concern). However, the natives decided to let it be for the moments to wait and see. Perhaps thing will be ok later if they (settlers) all settle in with their families.

Unfortunately, thing did not get better, in fact, they got worse over the years. Land ownership was confusing the Natives, while the Settlers were gaining more lands as time goes by.

President Joseph Jenkins Roberts, Administration was gaining ground and things were moving, government was expending, population was growing, business was going, land owner shipment was improving. The young republic was striving, things were moving in sequence. Except the natives were worry, not knowing what was going on at the moments. They managed to hold on for some times, but things got worse and worse for the natives. So they (the Chiefs) decided to meet with the government and people of the new republic to find out what was happening concerning the land issues and the settlers discriminatory behavior towards the natives. Unfortunately, the dispute did not go well between the two parties, because the settlers claim that the land was given to them and they had the right to build and fence their properties as they please to protect them and their kids from scavengers. The natives on the other hand felt disappointed and disgusted at the treatments of these (so-call brothers and sisters) from America. Based on this gross disregards of the natives feelings and concerns, the natives again decided to approach the issue in another way. They (the natives) got various chiefs together to formulate a new strategy of how to resolve these issues. They came up with an idea to take their issues to the new president, yet again to no availed. Because the president was busy running his government and making arrangements to settle his brother and sisters from America and other Caribbean Islands settlers that are moving back to the free land. The (natives) issues were dismissed as it was with the rest of the settlers. A complete belligerent exhibition to the native concerns.

"What do we do now" the natives cry, "give them a lot, (a piece of land) and they grow it to an Acres". Not stopping there, they were determined to take over the whole land and own it for they and their brothers, sisters and so-called Cousins. The natives felt helpless, so they decided to result into what they knew best, War! (If all else failed), and as they were already used to tribal wars. So, going to war to settle dispute was not strange to them. Because, they had fought and settled many battles before between the tribes. But this time it was against the invaders, so they had to approach this battle in a different way, cause the invaders are not the same kind of enemies they were used to. They were also aware that these people have different kinds of weapons called guns.

For this reasons, the natives gather their fighting gears and most fearful warriors to prepared for war against the invaders. The sad reality was, their weapons were no match for the settlers weapons. Guns compared to spears along with bow and arrow are no match at all, (one is a long range, and the other is a close encounter). But yet, a fight is a fight, no need turning back back now, the natives assured themselves that they were going through with the fight any way. Defending the rights of their people, and the land of their forefathers is a must. The stage was set, as things including (commodities) were getting high for the natives. But they could not stand by on the side line of their own country while the settlers take everything that belongs to them. So, they picked a time when and where to strike. They attacked the supply chain for the settlers to stop the supply of salt and other imports to the country. They also attacked the settlers homes to demand their land back. This did not sit well with the settlers, fear and chaos erupted amounts the settlers. "What is going on" they wonder. Little did they know that the natives would do this to them. "We are going to fight back" the settlers chanted, "who are those Scavengers that are trying to ruin our existing in this country". Subsequently, it was war, between the natives and the settlers. But the sad reality was, the settlers had an upper hand over the natives, because Uncle Sam (American Government) was still protecting the settlers. So, they (the settlers) called for help, to help them against the natives, because they were completely out number by the natives. For some strange reason, the (American Colonization Society) felt that they were obligated to the Free Slave that were sent to Africa. So (ACS) extended help to the settlers by sending arms and ammunitions to help the settlers in their fight against their enemies. (apparently ACS- felt the need not to let settlers down). As a result., they felt they were obligated to the settlers to make sure their mission is accomplished by helping.

ACS was already helping the settlers financially, so it was no brainer to give more help. By protecting their existing in this African nation to survive.

The big guns including "Cannon" were send out to help the settlers in their fight with the natives. The war lasted for many years (according to History- A female Settler, name Matilda Newport, was the one that shot the Cannon-Big Gun on the native). One of the defining factors in winning the war against the Natives in favor of the Settlers. She was celebrated as a National Hero, and a day was also set aside to be celebrated as a National Holiday on December 1, 1916 until it was abolished later by President William R. Tolbert Jr.). The Cannon, was the defining moment for the war, because it killed so many natives at one time. For this reason, the native had to give in to the war and accept defeat, because there were so many of them dying at one time from the Cannon. Again the natives felt helpless, because they have tried everything that they knew how to, to no avail. Giving up in the fight was not an easy thing, but they had to do what they had to do to save the life of their brothers and sisters. Compromised was the last option to save lives and accept peace. All the natives wanted was acceptance and inclusion in their own land, but that was difficult for the settlers to accept, because they (the natives) were consider country or ignorant, not civilized and not fit to be included in any thing that has to do with reading, writing or work for the government except domestic workers, people to work in the field, office boy, load carriers (in other words, they were not consider citizens on their own land), Mini-Apartheid idea. Domestic work and other non essential positions or jobs were allocated to natives including constructions and other odd jobs for many years.

CHAPTER THREE

THE FORMATION OF THE DEFENSE FORCE

The Militia was the first Defense Organization activated in Liberia on August 31, 1832 by Jehudi Ashmun, Agent of the Colony. Today, the modern Armed Forces of Liberia has its origin in the Liberia Frontier Force (LFF) in the administration of President Arthur Barclay in 1908 which comprised of 500 men who mission was originally to "patrol the borders in the hinterland (against British and French territorial expansions), and to prevent disorder. The "Frontier Force" is also known as Tax collectors. The Liberia Frontier Force became the Liberian National Guard later in 1965. The concept of the formation of the Liberian National Guard was to transition from Tax collector to the provision of national security for the citizens and residents of Liberia. The Liberian Military grew into fame by its participation in the United Nations backed peace-keeping mission in the Republic of Congo. The Liberian Government contributed 5 contingents which were attached to the Nigerian Brigade. The 1st. contingent was under the command of then Colonel Henry Korboi

Johnson. The 3rd. Contingent landed in Congo on August 1, 1961 under the command of Colonel James Dean. The 5th contingent landed in Congo on October 2, 1962 and remain until the final pull out of the Liberian Peacekeepers on March 16,1963. The Liberia National Guard became the Armed Forces of Liberia in 1970. The Navy, the Air Reconnaissance Unit and the Infantry were the three units developed. Before February 25, 1955 there as no Armed Forces Day in Liberia, except the country's Militia Units, which had its own quarterly parade day enacted by law of Liberia. (A day formerly known as "Old Soldier Army Festival"), a day on which units of Liberian Armed Forces throughout the nation would assemble at their respective headquarters to jointly participate in field ceremonies of parades and other planned military exercises. After some considerations over the years, to have the country set aside one day in a year to celebrate the Army as one unit, the legislature when to work.

February 11, 1909 was finally declared Armed Forces Day, but it was after bitter arguments - about Major Mckay Cadell incidence (insurrection) in 1909. (Major Mckay Cadell), was the first commandant of the Liberian Frontier Force who carried on mutiny action against the Liberian Government during President Arthur Barclay's Administration. That aggression of Cadell was repelled by the first Militia regiment headed by Ltc. Isaac Moart and his Deputy Major). At first, the amendment was made March 22, 1956 by the National Legislature declaring May 9 as Armed Forces Day; later deleting May 9 and inserting February 9 in the act as Armed Forces Day. Less than a year after the amendment was made, some survivors of the Major Cadel's incidence remember that the actual day was February 11, 1909. Once more the day was finally move to February 11, on January 26, 1957.

Armed Forces of Liberia, the primary function of this military assembly in Liberia is to defense, protect citizen and property. But, on the contrary, the Armed Forces was used has security guard for the official of government homes, businesses etc. Because since the Peace Keeping mission of 1962, Liberia have not had any other strategic mission or confrontation with other country pertaining to military aggression or invasion. So the Army was just a (lane duck) waiting for something to happen. Meanwhile, the elite (so-called civilize) big-shops comprise of Americo- Liberian were enjoying life, mostly working in government and running businesses manipulating all aspects and monopolizing some. "Liberia is sweet" they claim "what a place to be" they acknowledged. Life for the Americo-Liberian was fruitful, (even one of the Presidents, William R. Tolbert Jr., of Liberia at the time had on the back of his seat in the Executive Mansion, with words like "Do Not Forget The Pioneer's Children"). Well, life was very enjoyable for them, as anyone could imagine. Sadly, the natives and their kids were feeling the crunch of poverty and rejections by the elites for many years. One of the major employment for the natives and their kids was the military (security guards), education level for recruitment was zero (o) requirements," come as you are, we will train you" that was the model at the time. So, there was influx of most young people seeking employment through the military to take care of they and their families. "Noco" as they were called, meaning no knowledge, you can join without prior knowledge. The other employment opportunity for the poor was domestic worker, cleaning houses, cooking, washing clothes, yard work and running errands for the elites and their kids.

Tax commissioner/ Tax collector, was one of the job designated for some of the natives that could read or write English, mostly are escorted by one or two "Nocos" into the hinterland to collect "Hut Tax" from his own native people. Because the elites will not send anyone of their own to collect Taxes for fear of the natives attacking them. During that time, going to the interior part of the country to collect Taxes was very dangerous, risky and one has to have their own provision or be self-sufficient. For this reason, they have to take luggages along for sleeping and Tax bags that will be used for money as well as other goodie that come along on the road. Therefore, more help would be needed for the trip, but no worries because, they will get the help along the way from local government officials that were appointed by the County Superintendent in that region. Town chiefs are responsible for these tasks. (young men in those Towns carried their loads from Town to Town), that was the norm.

On the Tax collection missions, lots and lots of things happen along the way, mostly of things that were not transparent. (like sleeping with native women, tax collector being carry by young men on their shoulders in Hamon from town to town, on the the Tax collector's mission). More things were collected by the Tax collector on his or her mission that would not reach back to the city. Majority of the things collected on the road would be consumed by the Tax collector and his guards. Only fraction of the proceeds collected on the road will reach the city; all at the expanse of the indigenous people in the hinterland, who paid those Taxes and other collateral assets. This notion was perfectly known and understood by all Authorities concern. (there's no check and balance on what happens on the Tax collector's mission, it was a known benefits for Tax collectors). Collecting Taxes from the Indigenous People was not an easy thing both for the Collectors and the people they were getting the Taxes from. It was very difficult on both sides, but again the government's collector/s have the upper hand, because they have Guards, (Noco) with him or her to carry on the mission. Refusal to pay or don't have money to pay $10.00 USD per Hut. It was a punishable offense, and the treatment for that head of household is at the discretion of the Tax collector. (Some times those treatments were very crucial for the offender, most times it could be excruciating pain like lye flat on your back for hours to watch to watch the sun go down order by the Tax collector). The only crime could be, the head of house hold can not afford to pay the $10.00, especially for someone with no income. Even the ones that could afford to pay the $10.00, yet their Taxes were not beneficial to them and their families, nothing was awarded to them. Like road developments, Public schools and other amenities subsidized by government were not affordable to the indigenous and their kids. (No school bus, meals, text books, and other essentials), the indigenous have to make provisions on their own. (Abject Poverty), was the norm. "Only the Strong Survive". Oh yes, I do understand those pains,. I know what it means to walked about five miles one way under the Sun and under the rain to go to school, with no meal for (recess). If you don't come prepare with your food, you are out of luck., (and what luck has to do with hunger?). I am a descendant of the indigenous people, and most indigenous descendants can relate to this testimony. "Privilege" - is out of your vocabulary in those days, if you are a native's child. Life was very extreme under those conditions.

President William vs. Tubman & President J.F.K.

President William R. Tolbert & President Jimmy Carter

CHAPTER FOUR

DYNASTY, DAYS OF THE ELITES

Here is the Chronology of key events before the country went into Cruse Control: 1847 Constitution modeled on that of the U.S. Constitution was drawn up—(Easy copy, no brain storm by the settlers).

July 26, 1847 -Liberia became independent. May 8, 1917 Liberia declares war on Germany, by giving the Allies a base in West Africa during World War 1. 1926 Firestone Tire and Rubber Company opens rubber plantation on land granted by the Liberian government. Rubber production became backbone of economy for America and -(not one rubber factory in Liberia today). 1936 Forced- Labour abolished (after years of back breaking labor work by the poor). 1943 William V.S. Tubman elected president- (for 27 long years with no adequate developments- his usual phrase was "do you know who am I" meaning, you better recognize me). Smoking Cigar at the same time in your face. 1944 Government declares war on the Axis powers. (Axis

Powers - coalition headed by Germany, Italy, and Japan that opposed the Allied powers in World War II). May 1951 women and indigenous property owners voted in the presidential elections. (what's the point of participating in the election, - it was one party system in Liberia at the time. Most of the so-called parties were submerged by the leading and most dominant political party (True-Whig Party.). 1958 Racial discrimination outlawed - (yet civil discrimination persisted, and was very well alive) 1971 President Tubman died and was succeeded by Vice President William R. Tolbert Jr. (The saga continues with a new face). 1979 The Rice Riot happened and more than 40 people were killed following the proposed increase in the price of Rice Liberia's stable food. (It was the beginning of the end of the Dynasty). The two most influential presidents of Liberia in the late nineteenth century were, President William V.S. Tubman and, President William R. Tolbert Jr. They both help to change the dynamics of the political and economics trajectory of the country. They both had different views on how the country should be portray internationally and also change the prospective of the citizens and the perception of the Liberian people, but it was little too late. Because the people were already embedded into the "let's enjoyed" perspective. (Fuel for corruption), perpetuation of Liberia's problems.

President William V.S. Tubman (born November 29,1895 - July 23, 1971), was elected president 1944 until his death in 1971. For Liberia being the only free republic in Africa at the time, it was served as a model for African colonies struggling to achieve independence. Further, it highlighted the country's profile by traveling abroad and allowing International investors and investment in Liberia. Investment and the income from the newly discovered mineral deposits, helped president Tubman modernized parts of Liberia (mostly along the coast) and build schools, roads, and hospitals. He also expanded the cooperation of indigenous populations into the social and economic mainstream, granting them the right to vote. President Tubman was also instrumental in making Liberia a founding member of the United Nations as well as the Organization of African Unity (OAU). Despite these developments the gap between the ruling elite and the indigenous populations increased. Tubman was criticized for being too influenced by the United States and its interests in the (fight against communism), and for repressing political opposition. Tubman's rule became gradually more authoritarian. He changed the constitution to allow himself to remain in office for seven consecutive terms, gaged the press, and introduced a system of government spies to report on all political activity. His successor and former Vice President to him, Mr. William R. Tolbert Jr. tried to change the dynamic by toning down from what it used to be, after the death of president Tubman. His attempt was to improve the economic and political climate by introducing many new changes. But the political and economic climates in Liberia was too far gone to the left, the damage was already done by Tubman's Administration of which Tolbert was a part of. So, the Liberian people felt that Tolbert administration was just a continuation of Tubman doctrine and they were fed up with the status quo. They wanted real change.

President Tolbert did tried to make some changes in the economic and social wellbeing of the people by introducing a policy called "Total involvement for higher highs" Meaning, self-sufficient, especially with regards to the production of food. He wanted Liberian to help themselves to stop depending on import of food from foreign countries. But that did not work, especially when he increased the price of rice (the most consumed product) from $9.00 per 100 lbs. to $21.00 per 100 lbs., that was a steep rise for most of the people below poverty line.

Imagine someone (civil service worker) earning $30.00 a month, rent $10.00 per month and food (rice $21.00 for a 100 lbs. bag .). Well, do the math. This is why majority of the population were angry and frustrated about the situation at the time. President Tolbert's popularity became to demolished, lots of people dislike him including kids. Chaos and confusions began to set in both within his administration and the public. Allegedly, at one incident, kids were throwing stones at him on some occasions. (Frustrated at the fact that their parents will not be able to feed or sent them to school). Unfortunately, things were tumbling down for the Liberian leader. More over, when this political aspiring activist name, Gabriel Bacchus Matthews, Leader of The Progressive Alliance of Liberia (staged a peaceful protest against high cost of living for the common people, and advocated for decreased in the price of rice). With these demands by Mr. Matthews, from the government of Liberia to tone down the hardship for the common citizens. That demand did not go well with government. As a result, they order that Mr. Matthews be arrested. That incident started the rice riot in Liberia. Known as "April 14, 1979 Rice Riot" in the Liberians history. Subsequently, Mr. Matthews was arrested days later along with his followers and locked up. Charged with "Treason" against the government. Others were implicated but were not charge, due to their good standing or tied to government officials.

Tensions were high in the country, everybody was on edge not knowing what was going to happen to the political prisons that were lock up. It was also announced later in that year, that the prisons will go on trial on April 14, 1980 the following year. But the rumors was going around in the country that the political prisoners will be killed if they are found guilty as charged. Treason is punishable by death according to the law. Everything was quiet for a moment waiting for that trial day to come. After a year later, April came back so was the tension, fear and anxiety right where it all started. April 14, 1980 was the trial date. But before that day, something big, I mean very big that had changed the history of Liberia forever. "Noco" (Armed Forces Men- the uneducated ones) lead by Master Sergeant Samuel Kanyon Doe overthrown the government of Liberia by a coup d' 'e tat, assassinated President William R. Tolbert on April 12, 1980. Birth of a new era. Days before the trial of the Native people's children that were considered political prisoners, who were immediately freed after the coup d"'tat overthrowing of the Tolbert's regime.

People's Redemption Council

CHAPTER FIVE

BIRTH OF A NEW ERA, P.R.C.

People's Redemption Council (P.R.C.). Comprised of 17 enlisted men from the Armed Forces of Liberia. Some of the P.R.C. men were friends and colleagues in the Armed Forces. The overthrown event in Liberia was a very popular revolution (especially for the indigenous Liberians). Yet it was also brutal towards some of the Americo-Liberians and their decedents.

Well it was not known, if it was an intentional revenge, or pure malice against the ruling class, that has yet to be proven. The (PRC) claimed they overthrow the government to save the lives of the political prisoners that were held captive against their will. Fear that they made had been kill if they were not rescued. However, after President Tolbert was assassinated, most of his cabinet ministers and other permanent government officials were executed publicly on one of the beach fronts behind the Military Barrack in the city of Monrovia. Repression after the fact was daunting to these "Noco", not knowing what to do next.

They had no prior knowledge of how to run a government. So they had to rely on the so-called college educated activists that were just rescued from the government prisons. It was Mr. G. Bacchus Matthews, Mr. Togbah Nat Tepoteah and others, to fill the void of vacate government positions. Their mission was to bring about social change in the country and to eradicate corruption, well; so they claim. The mechanism of the P.R.C. government structure was formulated, where Master Sergeant Samuel K. Doe (from the Krahn Ethic tribes) was selected as Chairman of the People's Redemption Council. Most of the members were assigned to the Capital Building to replaced the National Legislature after the constitution was suspended by the new government. Except one of the members that was chosen by all members of the council to be Commanding General of the military, his name was (Thmas G. Quiwonkpa) who was assigned to the Military Barracks to control the Army in case of any rebellion from any other military personnel that are loyal to the old regime. The formation and coalition of the government held together for some times, closed to a year before everything fell apart from within the government. Trust issues, fabrications, fear of repressions, revenge, ignorance and gliding egotistic characters amongst the members played a major factor in the division of the P.R.C. members and their associates that lead to the demise of the People's Redemption Council. Propaganda, lies, deceit, and fear lead the P. R. C. To fight against each other by accusing some members of plotting to overthrow the Chairman and seize power. Purely orchestrated by some outside forces that wanted the P.R.C. government to fail. They surely succeeded with all kinds of lies, news propaganda both local and over seas.

The P.R.C. Government did not fall right away, it took some time for that to happen. There were few transformations before the fall, because the Chairman (Samuel Doe) had other intentions to run for president of Liberia.

The first thing they did was to dissolved the PRC government and form the Interim government, where Samuel Doe, himself became the interim president until election was held 1985. Before election was held, lots of things happened. The People's Redemption Counsel government had lots of chaos and confusions amounts themselves from outside forces that cause the Counsels to killed some of its members. Others fled including Thomas G. Quiwokpa to safe his life. Prior to 1985 election, there was a coup attempt lead by former Commander Thomas G. Quiwokpa who fled the country few years earlier, came back to overthrow the PRC government. His reasons, "the PRC government deceived the Liberian people" he said, "the Liberian people deserved better and the government is a betrayal". Unfortunately, he did not succeed. His forces got crushed the same day, arrested and was killed by Samuel K. Doe loyal forces. Allegedly, Doe soldiers when to Nimby County (the home of Thomas G. Quiwokpa), and slaughter so many Nimba ethnic groups including putting kids in wells. Also, so many Nimba people fled the country for fear of reprisal due to Quiwokpa incident. Nimba tribes men were targeted by the Doe regime including Price Y. Johnson, one of the rebel warlord supporting the Charles Taylor rebel lead base that was against the Samuel K. Doe Government. The sad reality is, Samuel K. Doe, Prince Y. Johnson and Thomas G. Quiwonkpa all are from the same south east region. Who for some strange reasons was manipulated by the Charles Taylor revenge mechanism strategy to fight with each other to fuel his political agenda. The strategy did work in Charles Taylor's favor. Because, Prince Y. Johnson and his rebel forces interrupted President Samuel Doe and the peace keeping (Ecomos) Commander at the Freeport of Monrovia, where Doe went to honor the invitation of the Peacekeeping Commander. September 9, 1990 to be exact that's when Doe was captured after killing all his bodyguards in Freeport. Prior to his demise, President Samuel K. Doe was torture and video tape for some hours before he was deceased. The death of Samuel K. Doe did not decrease the war, in fact it did intensified the war between all tribal groups in Liberia, especially between the Krahn and Gio ethic groups. Killings were going on by Samuel K. Doe supporter lead by Major General Namina of the Krahn tribe and Prince Y. Johnson of the Gio tribe.

The brutal killings between those tribes were so unbearable to the point that some factions were eating human remains for food,(Cannibalism). Those dehumanizing activities lasted for few years while Charles Taylor, the main instigator of the war in Liberia's Civil War. Finally decided to come with reinforcement from his Headquarter in the Southeastern Region (Gbanga city) to Monrovia city to sweep both factions to take over power by captioning the Executive Mansion, the headquarters of the presidency. Unfortunately, he too encounter resistance from the Krahn ethic group loyal to Samuel K. Doe. They did not permit him to enter the Executive Mansion. Frustrated by the resistance of the Krahn ethic groups, Charles Taylor decided to joined forces with Prince Y. Johnson to crushed the Krahn ethic forces that were denying him the right to take over the Mansion. With both warlords joined together to fight the Krahn Forces, yet they could not defeat the Krahn fearless forces who were prepared to die at all cost, because their backs were against the Atlantic Ocean with no where else to run for refuge or safety. So, resistance was the only way out of extermination. "Move it" as they chanted, running to the enemies with little or nothing to fight with. (Remember "it's not the size of the dog in the fight, but the size of the fight in the dog"). Because, no one wants to feel helpless if he or she is face with death or extermination. The Krahn people had to do what they had to do to fight back. They did not win the war, but they won the fight. They were not slaughter by the enemy forces. Most of the Krahn people survive the war and live to tell the story today. An ultimate survivor story in the midst of chaos and confused war.

Charles G. Taylor
Rebel Leader

CHAPTER SIX

PEOPLE'S REDEMPTION COUNCIL DOWNFALL

Revolution means change, either absolute change or radical change for a better result of whatever it should be. P.R.C. did not understand these concepts. They took over the government with one track mind only to free the political prisoners that were held captive by the Tolbert's Regime. There was no plans in place to form a government better yet run it. All they wanted was to take over, free the prisons and seize power. At first everything seen so unbelievable to the entire nation including the PRC members that took over the government. However, their bravery actions broke the walls of discriminations and the yoke of oppressions against the Natives by the Americo-Liberians. The country was overwhelm with Jubilation by majority of the population especially the natives, the oppressed people. Contrary to this happiness, the children and families of the old regime were worried with fear of what would become of them after the jubilation is settle. To make matter worse, 13 members of the Tolbert's government were executed publicly on the beach by firing squad without proper investigations. They were charged with Rampant Corruption, Human Right abuse and miss used of public properties. (they were not given any chance to defend themselves). Consequently, the PRC government was already doom before it got started. Because there were so much hatred and animosity from all sides of the aisle including the natives. Reason being, Liberia is a closed nest society. Everybody is inter-related due to the nature of the country's culture.

One of the key factors, was the inter-related marriages amongst the (Americo-Liberian and the natives). Besides, most natives had personal connections with majority of the Americo-Liberians. Some native kids were raised by most Congo people, others were connected by school backgrounds. So, by putting those 13 former officials on firing squad was the wrong thing they did that led to the demise of the P.R.C. Government, or perhaps the beginning of the end.

Days after the execution of those 13 former officials, the jubilations, and rejoicing atmosphere subsided into fear, confusion and anger. People were confused didn't know what next, who next. The whole country was in a confused state. "What is going on, what do we do next" the citizens were wondering, didn't know what was going to be the next move of the PRC government. Despite the chaos and confusion in the country, the PRC ignored all that. They when ahead and appointed people in positions to form a new government. Some of the appointments were the very people that were released from prison (former political prisoners) that were Held captive from the old regime. Worse of all, their cabinet appointments included some former officials children, a recipe for disaster. Unfortunately, they had no other alternative. Instead, they included the children of the former regime into the government because, most of the Americo-Liberians were educated and experience. Majority of the native kids were not educated and could not fit into those positions. So, the dilemma was how to fill the cabinet positions that were left to be fill. For this reason, the PRC government had no other choice but to bring in the children of the Americo-Liberians and former regime offspring to fill those positions. (A complete recipe for disaster to the PRC government that lead to its down fall). Reason been, you can not kill a man by firing square and turn around and hire his sons and daughters to work with you, "HOW, WHY". Who does that, (it is like drinking a poison, and hoping it does not kill you). That's what the PRC government was hoping for, but the end result is, poison kills. (Lucky if you make it to the hospital in time. Unfortunately, the PRC did not make to to hospital in time.).

When they (PRC) hired some decendents of the former officials, including Charle K. Taylor and others, the stage was set for deceptions. The "pioneers' children" (as they were sometimes referred to), when to work and staring to undermined the People's Redemption Counsel. The first step was to create fear and confusion within the Council, by spreading propaganda amongst members and other officials of the P.R.C. government. Say that "some members of the Council were plotting to overthrow the Chairman (Samuel K. Doe). The news when like wild fire within the PRC government and the nation in general. Fear, confusion and chaos grace the nation that resulted into a brutal killing 5 five Council Members that were falsely accused of the plot to overthrow Doe. Subsequently, the entire nation was in a confused state again. No body knows what to do or what was going on, meanwhile, Charle Taylor and others were stealing money from the government and finding their way out. After the dust settled then the PRC government finally realized, Charle Taylor, the Government Services Agency -GSA Director, allegedly stole $1.4 millions from the Government Services Agency (GSA) budget of which he was a Director. Money allegedly used later to recruit and pay people to come back to Liberia to overthrow the People's Redemption Council Government. He became a warlord purposely to redeem the Pioneers' children and restored Americo-Liberians legacy. Oops too late, the walls were broken and there's no turning back now. He met up with some resistance, even though he managed to get his aim accomplished by getting Doe out of power, but the war was already won by Master Sergeant Samuel Kanyon Doe. (you can kill a person with a dream but you can not kill the dream). Martin Luther King proves that.

Master Sergeant Doe was brutally murder on September 9, 1990 by Charles Taylor's accomplice Prince Y Johnson, (warlord) and a native born Liberian (both Doe and Johnson from the same "southeastern" region) killing one another only because they were manipulated by these Americo-Liberians, claiming they came back to rescue the Liberian people from mass killing and misappropriation of Liberia's economy. Forgetting to know that regime change does not solve the economic problems in Liberia. His main intentions were to bring back the old rules of the Americo-Liberians legacy, let Congo peoples' rule again policy. He did not rest, few years later after the war seized, especially after the intervention of the ECOWAS and the International Communities. Charles Taylor decided to contest in the up coming Election mandated by ECOWAS and the International World after the 15 years of war in Liberia. Reluctantly, most Liberia voted for Charles Taylor, (only to avoid more bloodshed in case if he does not win). Chanting - "you kill my mom, you kill my papa I will vote for you" completely out of desperation for peace. The 1995 election declared Charles Taylor winner, but the carnage did not stopped. The brutal killings still continues especially by Charles Taylor loyalist against his opposition and people that opposed him. Which means the war still continues under Charles

Taylor's ruled. Those atrocities lasted for few more years until it came to the breaking point that dead bodies of women and children where been display in front of the United States Embassy in Liberia. Thereby initing human rights uproar worldwide accusing United States of America of paying death ears to Liberia's problems. Due to the negative publicity and human right abuses that were going on in Liberia, United States President at the time Mr. George W. Bush had to react to those bad news by giving order to the Liberian President Mr. Charles Taylor to "leave Liberia immediately or else". After this order from President George W. Bush, few days later Charles Taylor was force to leave Liberia in 2003. The end result of Charles Taylor today is 50 years in prison for war crime, human right abuse and blood diamond incidents in Sierra Leone West Africa. (Where women and children were brutally murder, mutilated and displaced in orphanage homes and refugee camps).

CHAPTER SEVEN

NEW BEGINNING/ OLD WINE IN A NEW BOTTLE

After the departure of Charles Taylor from Liberia, an interim government was set up to make way for a new beginning in the post civil war era. A beginning with a newly drafted constitutions for all Liberians to exercise their political rights. The transitional government lasted for 2 two years to set the stage for a democracy government to be elected in the country. On November 23, 2005, Ellen Johnson Sirleaf was declared the winner of the Liberian election and confirmed as the country's next president and the first woman to be elected as president of an African country. Her inauguration took place on 16 January 2006. She came to power with such an impressive resume; She began her career in the Treasury Department in Liberia in 1965. In 1979, she rose to the position of Minister of Finance and introduced measures to curb the mismanagement of government finances. When the 1980 coup d'stat happened, she was one of those that were considered to work with the People's Redemption Councils' government including Charles Taylor. Where she held the position as president of the Liberian Bank for Development and investment, but fled Liberia that same year, escaping an increasingly suppressive military government. Mrs. Sirleaf also served as Vice President of Citicorp's African regional office in Nairobi, Kenya as a senior Vice President for Equator Bank. In addition to her qualifications, she also served as assistant administrator of the United Nations Development Program personel as well as Director of its Regional Bureau of Africa with the rank of Assistant Secretary-General of the United Nations. A post she resigned later to contest for her first presidential election in 1997 in the heat of the civil war. Unfortunately, she came second in the election behind Charles Taylor. After coming in second, she went into self-imposed exile in a neighboring country Côte d'Ivoire for some time.

Ellen Johnson Sirleaf surfaced again in 2005 to contest for the general election again where she finally won the election and she became the 1st. Female president in Africa, particularly Liberia. It was all because of her international influence, an incredible educational background from Harvard University combined with her Global connections. Obviously, she was the chosen one, not only for the presidency of Liberia but to also bring peace back to Liberia after the 15 years of a brutal civil war. Ellen Johnson Sirleaf, election and presidency was a no brainier, everyone in Liberia needed a breath of fresh air to bring back stability. Amazingly, it was the opposite. Her government was more corrupt and divisive than the previous administrations combined. During her tender, the international communities including the Uniter States of America contributed 4 Billions US$ to her government to help with reconstructions, developments, reconciliations and peacekeeping initiatives. Most especially to heal the warns of a nation. And to also provide opportunities for the most vulnerable youths of the country, the future leaders. Sadly, those objectives were never met for 12 years during her tender. Yet she was awarded "Noble Peace Prize" for what peace?, this has yet to be defined. Instead, she awarded her families with lavish lifestyle to live comfortably after she leaves office as they are right now. While poverty, depression and hunger are killing Liberians young and old. To make matter worse, Ellen did not support her Vice President that had been with her for 12 years, Mr. Joseph Buakia to succeed her. Either she was afraid he made had exposed her corrupt deals or bring her to face court prosecution of corruption and mismanagement charges. Instead, she supported an opposition party candidate, a flamboyant playboy who also happen to be an international soccer star name George Weah. Even though, Ellen Johnson Sirleaf served as president of Liberia from (2006-2017), being the first female elected head of state of an African country. Some of her biggest accomplishments were, she secured millions of dollars of foreign investment and also wept out millions of dollars debt owned by the Liberian government. She also established a Truth and Reconciliation Committee to probe corruption and heal ethnic tensions after the war. A commission she later ignored after the submission of findings that somehow implicated her in some of the crimes. Ellen is unpredictable, she was perceived as a savior for Liberia, but her actions prove otherwise. Hopes and dreams were crushed compensated with despair and disappointments."What do we do now", cried the Liberian people. They felt the walls were closing in on them when Ellen terns was about to be over. (War was the first and the last thing on their minds).

With no hope of who to rely on, again the Liberian people were vulnerable. Not knowing who or what to believe anymore, so the people decided to wait and see. The political arena was filled with lots of aspirant candidates. After Ellen's two terns were over in 2017. One of the contestants that emerged from the rest was this professional footballer who is affectionately known amongst the Liberia people and most of Africa as; "World Best" Mr. George M. Weah. He contested vigorously for the position of President. With the help of his international status and a local hero affiliation with the youth of the country, he managed to secured a seat with his political party as a standard bearer contesting for the presidential position. Especially coming from a Senate seat in the National Legislative Breach of government to contest was a plus. Despite the overcrowded political fields, George M. Weah was exceptionally popular amongst his people compared to most of his opponents. In-fact, one of his opposition candidate (Mrs. Jewel Howard Taylor) joined his Party to run with him as a Vice Presidential candidate. More over, the out going president (Hon. Ellen Johnson Sirleaf) who is also from an opposition party, endorsed his candidacy for president. As a result, overwhelming majority of the population voted for him on Election Day (67%) to award him the presidency. It was a landslide victory for Mr. Weah. January 22, 2018 was Hon. George Manneh Weah Inauguration Day. On that day, the first paragraph of his inauguration Speech was, "My fellow citizens, I have spent many years of my life in stadiums, but today is a feeling like no other. Today, we all wear the jersey of Liberia, and the victory belongs to the people, to peace, and to democracy." Well as of now, history have yet to determine whether he will take the Liberian people to a better destination. Time will tell.

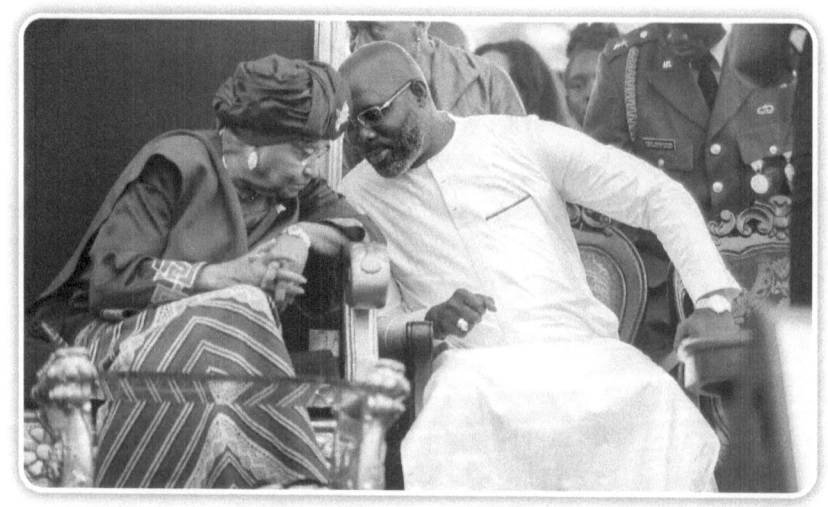

President Ellen Johnson Sirleaf & President George M. Weah

CHAPTER EIGHT

DESTINY UNKNOWN/ ARE WE THERE YET

Every beginning has an end, what goes up must come down, and million miles begin with one step. The question remains is; are we there yet, Liberians? I hope and pray that we make it there, where-ever there is. But before moving forward, we have to back track and understand where we are, what our mistakes are and our mission forward. Also, we have to evaluate our downfalls and problems areas. No one can solve a problem if you don't know what the problem is. Our problems are discrimination, (remnant of prejudicial treatment brought over by Americo -Liberians from America and other European countries), Second thing they did was big guns to destroy the Natives and (using America as a 2nd. Home for the free Slaves). Third thing is taking land from the Natives unknowingly with no remorse or reparation. Fourth thing is, Denying them education. Fifth and final thing is, stripping the natives of their culture heritage and traditional beliefs. (Same basic principle that were taking away from the slaves by their slave masters). Inhuman treatments that they were running away from in America and migrated to Africa, (they called themselves civilized people). How can you be civilized if you are treating other human being inhumanly. These attitudes and other human rights abuses lasted for 133 years until 1980 when the People's Redemption Council (coup d'e'-tat) broke the mode of oppressions and discriminations in Liberia. Yes, the PRC had their own shot-comings with the way they handle power, but they were only repeating what they learned from previous administrations before them. Remember, they were Noco's with no prior knowledge of educations,. So, they were ditching out what was given to them. A response of what happen when you don't educate your society and expect to get a good results. (Nope). It is not justifiable for the atrocities and human rights abuses that the People's Redemption Council committed during their regime. In-fact, it was a complete violation of human dignity and outright murders. But blames are share both ways on the past regimes as well with the PRC government. Oppression has consequences, there's no telling what anyone will do when they're given a chance over their oppressors. They say "revenge is sweet", but another statement also says, "two wrongs don't make it right". Well, it is time to move on because lives matter, it doesn't matter whose right or wrong. Everyone's life is important.

Recovery after war starts with reconciliation and forgiveness. A very hard thing to do, but resolution starts somewhere. Mostly from the heart comes with compassion combined with action to forgive. Oftentimes, it hurts to let go of feelings that are sentimental to us. However, revenge can destroy a nation because, it can escalade to more violent one after another. Generation revenging on generation can lead to total destruction, the same devastation that Liberia is face with today. How do we rise above this kind of set back that took us 50 back years. Well, change is necessary sometimes only if we recognize where we went wrong. This is what Liberians need to know before going back to the drawing board. Right now everybody is hurting regardless of congo or country, we are in this together. Only us (Liberians) can lift the image of Liberia back on the World stage. We are resilient people, remember we were once on the top of the hill in Africa (Liberia was name small "America in Africa"). I believe we can get there once more. Only if we show care and compassion for one another, most especially being patriotic to the country, (Liberia).

I believe we can do it if we try. Great nations have recovered from their ugly past, like America, China, Nigeria, Rwanda, and many other nations have done it, why not Liberia. One of the biggest problem that had perpetuated throughout in Liberia from generation to generation is failure to love the country call Liberia. This blame goes mainly to the founding fathers of Liberia (Americo-Liberia). Because their roots were from America and the American way of life as part of their adopted culture, this is why they wrote on the Seal; "The love of Liberty brought us here". Well, (The love of liberty met us here) .. The point is how do we get alone to rebuild the sweet land of Liberty (Liberia). No body else that is going to do it for us, but us. So, I am appealing to all Liberians to do something. John F. Kennedy once said "Ask not what your country can do for you, but what you can do for your country". If we (Liberians) have that concept about Liberia the country will be a better place. Let's teach one another what we know and share with one another. My fellow Liberians, believe that Liberia belongs to all Liberians. You do not owned anything in America, European countries or elsewhere, you are only renting whatever it is. Please understand your roots, perhaps it will help you to know who you are. Because no one will respect you if don't know who you are or the significant of your background. (Understand this, if a man knows how valuable your background is, he will respect you on a dinner table).

Russian President Vladimir Putin said it best; "Africa is a cemetery for Africans, they present themselves as weak people, especially when dealing with Europeans and Americans, they are their own enemies, they hate each others, that gives the colonies power to continuous exploration of their resources. When an African begin rich, his bank account in Swaziland, travel to France for medical treatments, he rest in Germany, he buys from Dubai, they consumed Chinese, he travel to Europe for tourism, when he died his body will be taken to Africa for buried".

Liberia is the land of liberty that belongs to all Liberians and we have to protect it by all cost. It doesn't matter if you are Congo or Country, the only thing that we should all be concern about is the **"love of liberty"** for all. Because the sad reality is, foreigners come to Liberia and they enjoy the country better than Liberians that owned the birth rights to the land. Mineral resources exploited, US currency taken away, business opportunities manipulated by foreign nationals. For almost 200 years, common Liberians have yet to feel that they belong to the society and the land of liberty. Liberia's biggest problem and the sole deficiency of this country issue is governess, (wrong people in power). The sad truth is, everyone's in power wants to enrich himself and his families. A total disregard to everyone including the young generation, the future leaders of tomorrow. We have to erase that concept, because the wealth of the country belongs to every Liberians. Other nations have done it and continue to do so for their people, why not us. Liberia is a rich nation with mineral resources; (Gold, Dimond, Timber, Iron ole, rubber plantation and copper). Why be name one of the poorest country in the World at # 7 on the list with $673 GDP per capital at 11.98% annual growth rate. Bob Marley said best, "In the abundance of water, a fool is thirsty". Why are we poor, if we have all these resources. Well, the answer is simple, we have to do critical thinking to elect or select the right people to lead us. LIBERIA BELONGS TO ALL LIBERIANS.

Liberians in Huts

Liberians Condition remain the same

CHAPTER NINE

RESOLUTIONS/ RECOMMANDATIONS

Every conflict has a resolution, and most problems have solutions. A peaceful resolution starts with an open communication, along with an active listener. Also, a resolution consider other people opinions that may be beneficial to everyone. The exception to Liberia's problems that have perpetuated for this length of time (173 years to be exact) is, the concept of "enjoyment"; once a Liberian man gets in power, the next thing is "it is my time to enjoy", a complete disregard to everyone's birth rights over the country's resources.. Perception, and the ability to see things with a different lens or vision is Liberians' biggest challenge. Perhaps, the most reviewing obstacle to Liberia's progress is changing the mind set of the people. They need to understand that the resources of the country belongs to every citizen of that country. Ignorance and corruptions is detrimental to any society especially an under-develop country like Liberia. Imagine stealing from the poor to feed the rich, awkward and stupid. Unfortunately, that's what Liberians do to their own country, why? The concept is beyond belief, but this is why Liberia remains poor since the country was founded almost 200 years ago. Trajectory, perception, deception, corruption and unpatriotic attitude have to be change towards a better behavior of how we treat one another and the country for a profound Liberia that we all can be proud of in this World. Liberians are resilient people, when we show up, we will show out to make our presence known. During the Civil War in Liberia, and the citizens of Liberia were displaced around the world, it was proven that Liberians dominated in all aspects of social scene, with a commanding lead in the women cooking skills, dress code, passionate sense of humor, intelligent, open minded and very receptive to any conditions that prevailed itself to him or her regardless of the circumstances. The sad reality is, we are our own enemies. We tear one another down with no empathy or remorse, a defining factor to Liberia's failed progress. However, Liberians need to go back to visit the Creed of the country that held all Liberians accountable to support the Lone Star forever… "overseas and on land". Everyone should be involve into the country's business, Liberia for all Liberians. Be a patriotic Liberian, get involved (Foreigners are taking over, don't sit back and watch).

Lets recite Liberia National Anthem once again, perhaps it may re-energize our efforts to unify the country that we call the land of liberty.

{All hail, Liberia, hail!!!
All hail, Liberia, hail

This glorious land of liberty
Shall long be ours

Though new her name,
Great be her fame,
And mighty be her powers

In joy and gladness with our hearts united,
    We'll shout the freedom of grace benighted,

Long live Liberia, happy land!
    A home of glorious liberty,

By God's command !!
    All hail, Liberia, hail!!
    All hail, Liberia, hail!!

In union strong success is sure
    We cannot fail!!

With God above our rights to prove
    We will o'er all prevail,
    We will o'er all prevail,

With heart and hand
    Our country's cause defending

We'll meet the foe with valor unpretending

Long live Liberia, happy land!
    A home of glorious liberty, by God's command

A home of glorious liberty, by God's command!!}

Liberty for all.

To all Liberians, I challenge you to make Liberia the shinning "Star" once again in Africa!!!! "All hail, Liberia, hail" ….

AUTHOR'S BIO

Alex Dougbowea Tarlue, a native of Liberia, who has a Degree in Business Administration from the University of Phoenix, an Air Craft Mechanic Certificate from the Aviation Institute of Maintenance, Philadelphia, Pa., a Certified HVAC Contractor. Who also works at the Children Hospital of Philadelphia as a Building Maintenance Engineer. He has five children; Prince, Anita Alex II, Kpadehee and Kimasa. Alex's hobbies include reading, writing, sports, telling stories, photography, and travel.

www.ingramcontent.com/pod-product-compliance
Lightning Source LLC
LaVergne TN
LVHW042247070526
838201LV00089B/61